Vincent
VAN GOGH

Paintings

WINGS BOOKS
New York · Avenel, New Jersey

Introduction
Copyright © 1992 by Outlet Book Company, Inc.

Published by Wings Books,
distributed by Outlet Book Company, Inc.,
a Random House Company,
40 Engelhard Avenue, Avenel, New Jersey, 07001.

Grateful acknowledgement is made to Superstock, Art Resource and The Granger
Collection for permission to use their transparencies of the artwork.

Printed and bound in Singapore

Library of Congress Cataloging-in-Publication Data

Gogh, Vincent van, 1853-1890.
  Vincent Van Gogh paintings.
    p.   cm.
  ISBN 0-517-07762-0
  1. Gogh, Vincent van, 1853-1890—Catalogs.   2. Miniature books—
Catalogs.   I. Title.
ND653.G7A4   1992a
759.9492—dc20   92-2725
                                                       CIP

8   7   6   5   4   3   2   1

I can think of no better definition for the word art than this: nature, reality, truth; but with a significance...a character which the artist brings out in it, and to which he gives expression.

—VINCENT VAN GOGH

1. *The Cypresses* 1889

2. *Sunflowers* 1888

3. *View of Arles with Irises* 1888

4. *Café Terrace at Night* 1888

5. *Starry Night Over the Rhone* 1888

6. *The Baby Marcelle Roulin* 1888

7. *L'Arleseinne: Madame Ginoux* 1888

8. *Memory of the Garden at Etten* 1888

9. *Vase with Irises* 1890

10. *The Potato Eaters* 1885

11. *Peasant Woman* 1885

12. *A Pair of Shoes* 1886

13. *Self-Portrait with a Bandaged Ear* 1889

14. *Seascape at Saintes Maries de la Mer* 1888

15. *Farmhouse at Cordeville* 1890

16. *The Night Café* 1888

17. *The Church at Auvers-sur-Oise* 1890

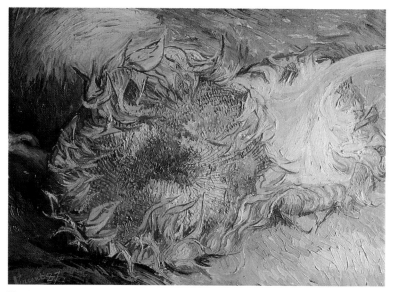

18. *Sunflowers* 1887

19. *Portrait of Dr. Gachet* 1890

20. *Imperial Crown Fritillaria in a Copper Vase* 1887

21. *Wheatfield with Lark* 1887

22. *Portrait of Pére Tanguy* 1887

23. *White Roses* 1890

24. *The Bedroom at Arles* 1889

25. *Trees in Front of the Asylum at Saint-Rémy* 1889

26. *Harvest Landscape with Blue Cart* 1888

27. *Postman Roulin* 1889

28. *Cornfield with Cypress Tree* 1889

29. *View of Arles* 1889

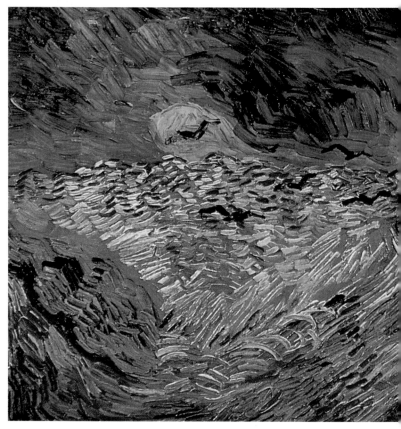

30. *Wheatfield with Crows* 1890

31. *The Siesta* 1889–90

Afterword

My own work, I am risking my life for it and my reason has half-foundered.[1]

With these words, Vincent Van Gogh ended his last letter to his brother Theo, his life-long confidant, who provided him not only with ungrudging financial support, but with the encouragement and love the artist so desperately needed. Van Gogh, who took his own life in July, 1890, had a career as a painter which lasted a scant ten years, a period of intense poverty, loneliness, and increasing mental decline. But during that period he created a legacy—more than 2,000 paintings and drawings—which is incalculable.

Born in Groot Zundert, Holland in 1853, the son of a vicar, Van Gogh was an intensely religious man. He spent his early manhood pursuing the religious life, first as a lay preacher in England, later as an evangelist among the miners of Belgium. He was a man of deep social consciousness, a reader of Shakespeare, Dickens, Hugo, and Harriet Beecher Stowe, who saw art as the way to create a social record of what he called "the universality of suffering."

I can think of no better definition for the word art than this: nature, reality, truth; but with a significance...a character which the artist brings out in it, and to which he gives expression....The miners and the weavers form a race apart...and I feel a great sympathy for them, and should be very happy if one day I could draw them.[2]

In early 1881, he returned to Holland and studied painting at The Hague with Anton Mauve until, after less than a month, a quarrel ended the lessons. For the next five years, Van Gogh moved from city to city, drawing and painting. In 1886 he joined his brother Theo in Paris, where Theo had opened a gallery devoted to the works of the Impressionists. Van Gogh's introduction there to Emile Bernard, Henri de Toulouse-Lautrec, Camille Pissaro, Georges Seurat, Paul Gaugin, and others would profoundly influence his work. The somber dark hues of his northern heritage were abandoned in favor of the luminous color of the Impressionist palate. Then, in February, 1888, Van Gogh, driven by a desire for seclusion and a need to escape the hectic pace of the Paris art world, fled to Arles in the south of France, where he would create his greatest masterpieces.

In Arles, Van Gogh discovered a "kingdom of light" and breathtaking color. It restored his sense of a mystical, creative force in the universe, a version of his early religious fervor. He worked with feverish energy:

When he comes as a foreigner to Arles...he paints everything—day and night scenes, people, children, whole families, cafés, streets, his own room, and the surrounding country—as if to enter completely into this new milieu....[3]

The most ordinary subjects were transformed by his passion. Writing to his brother about his painting "Bedroom at Arles", Van Gogh explained:

I had an idea in my head and here is the sketch to it...this time it's simply my bedroom, only here color is to do everything and, giving by its simplification a grander style to things, is to be suggestive of rest....In a word, to look at the picture ought to rest the brain or rather the imagination.[4]

Van Gogh became obsessed with the idea of creating an artist's community and prevailed upon Paul Gaugin to join him in Arles in the fall of 1888. Their constant companionship ended in a furious argument on December 23, after which, in a moment of self-recrimination, Van Gogh sliced off the lobe of his left ear. Gaugin left Arles the following day, declaring that his presence would further agitate Van Gogh, who thereupon suffered a severe breakdown. He was taken by the police to a mental hospital where he remained for two weeks. For the next several months, the artist had to be periodically confined in the Arles hospital, and he became conscious of the debilitating effects of his illness:

What comforts me is that I am beginning to consider madness as a disease like any other, and accept the thing as such, whereas during the crises themselves I thought that everything I imagined was real.[5]

His neighbors, frightened by his behavior, petitioned to have him committed, so in May of 1889, Van Gogh voluntarily entered the asylum at St. Rémy on the condition that he be allowed to continue to paint. Much of his time during this period was spent copying the works of others—Delacroix and Millet among them—transforming them with his invigorating sense of color. The year he spent at St. Rémy was interrupted by bouts of despair, but nonetheless Van Gogh completed 150 paintings and 100 drawings, including "Trees in Front of the Asylum at Saint Rémy", and "Vase with Irises" (plate 9), a final attempt to catch the serenity and color of the South.

At the beginning of 1890, after recovering from an unsuccessful suicide attempt, Van Gogh returned to Paris, writing to Theo, "The North appeals to me like a new country."[6] He visited Theo, then settled in Auvers-sur-Oise, where Dr. Paul Gachet, a specialist in nervous disorders and a friend of Theo's, could keep an eye on him. Again he threw himself into his work and in less than three months produced 83 canvases, including "Portrait of Dr. Gachet" (plate 19) and "The Church at Auvers-sur-Oise" (plate 17). But the terrors of his illness continued to haunt him, and on July 27, 1890, Van Gogh shot himself. He died the next day, with Theo at this side. His friend, the painter Emile Bernard, arrived for the burial, and in a letter poignantly described the scene:

> On the walls of the room where the body reposed, all his last canvases were nailed, making a kind of halo around him....On the coffin, a simple white drapery and masses of flowers, the sunflowers he so loved, yellow dahlias, yellow flowers everywhere. It was his favorite color...symbol of the light that he dreamed of finding in hearts as in artworks.[7]

Van Gogh had absorbed the lessons of the Impressionists, and adopted some of Seurat's pointillist techniques. In his hands, however, the brushstrokes, the patches of color, were imbued with an extraordinary emotionalism—and exaltation. Van Gogh wrote:

> The emotions are sometimes so strong that one works without being aware of working...and the strokes come with a sequence and coherence like the words in a speech or letter.[8]

The result is that his paintings achieve an effect nearly opposite those of the Impressionists. The Impressionists recorded nature passively, Van Gogh deformed it in order to interpret it. In that way his work seems closer to that of the Symbolists.

He instilled a trembling vibrancy into every motif. His subjects—the night sky, cypresses, fields—are imbued with a symbolic value. He tried to explain, "Cypresses which show off their nightmarish silhouettes of black flame; mountains which rear their backs like mammoths or rhinoceroses."[9] When he wrote Theo about 'Starry Night" (cover), he said,

> Why, I ask myself, shouldn't the shining dots of the sky be as accessible as the black dots on the map of France? Just as we take a train to reach Tarascon or Rouen, we take death to reach a star.[10]

Van Gogh reaffirmed the central importance of the human figure. Often, because he lacked money to hire models, he used himself. His self-portraits (plate 13) capture an inner reality that has led some historians to suggest that he was monitoring his mental stability in his many paintings of himself.

> I should like to paint portraits which would appear after a century to the people living then as apparitions.... I do not endeavor to achieve this by photographic resemblance but by means of our impassioned expressions—using our knowledge of and our modern taste for color.[11]

He manipulated the spectrum, not mimicking the colors of "reality", but choosing the colors that would somehow reveal the essential nature of his subjects. Van Gogh said, "I have tried with red and green to express the terrible human passions."[12] Julius Meier Graefe, who did much to establish the artist's reputation in Germany, wrote:

He risked the most dangerous combinations...but chose the quantities with such unerring skill as to make the most daring appear as though it were the most natural.[13]

All his choices were extreme: "Van Gogh always succeeded one notch beyond other artists: if he was dark like the Dutch, he was darker than they; if he was light and colorful like the French, he surpassed their brightness" (Johan de Meester).[14] And when he painted light, he was equally audacious. In "Café Terrace at Night" (plate 4), he shows both natural and artificial light, each individual, subtly different from the other.

He carried the sun in his head and a hurricane in his heart.... He did not paint with his hands but with his naked senses...painting himself within those fiery clouds...in those twisting trees that seem to yell to heaven, in the frightening vastness of his plains.[15]

Perhaps more than any other painter, Van Gogh put his state of mind into his art. The reverberations of his acute sensitivity range from the almost Oriental sublimity of his paintings of flowers (plates 2, 9, 23), to the nightmare-like mood of "Wheatfield with Crows" (plate 30), painted only a few days before his suicide. Its distorted perspectives seem to echo on canvas the artist's struggle for control.[16]

During his lifetime, Van Gogh sold only two pictures. His works, exhibited in 1889 and 1890, and in a retrospective mounted by Theo after his death, were generally greeted with ridicule or indifference. Today, his paintings sell for millions of dollars and he is among the best-known and most loved of all painters. His vision speaks clearly—and profoundly—to contemporary viewers.

Painting is...a matter of seizing the power, taking over from nature...Van Gogh was the one to find the key to that tension.

—Pablo Picasso[17]

NOTES

1. Irving Stone, editor, *Dear Theo* (New York: Signet Book), 480
2. Ibid, 41, 51
3. Meyer Schapiro, *Modern Art* (New York: George Braziller), 97
4. E. M. Gombrich, *The Story of Art* (Englewood Cliffs, New Jersey: Prentice Hall), 438
5. *Dear Theo*, 421
6. Massuni Gemin, *Van Gogh* (New York: Arch Cape Press), 18
7. Susan Alyson Stein, editor, *Van Gogh: A Retrospective* (New York: Park Lane), 220
8. *The Story of Art*, 436
9. William Feaver, *Van Gogh* (New York: Portland House), 28
10. Ibid, 106
11. Ibid, 128
12. René Huyghe, *Van Gogh* (New York: Crown Publishers), 47
13. *Van Gogh: A Retrospective*, 327
14. Ibid, 264
15. Ibid, 318
16. *Modern Art*, 89
17. *Van Gogh: A Retrospective*, 380

List of Plates

The photographs in this book were supplied by: